THE CARIBBEAN FAMILY

Jamaica Pen Publishers

Maryland, USA.

THE CARIBBEAN FAMILY

Understanding Family Diversity in the Caribbean

by:

Denise N. Fyffe

TABLE OF CONTENTS

ACKNOWLEDGMENT 7

CHAPTER 1: INTRODUCTION.......................8

CHAPTER 2: THE FAMILY 13

CHAPTER 3: TYPES OF CARIBBEAN FAMILIES 21

CHAPTER 4: THE IMPACT OF SLAVERY................29

CHAPTER 5: THE LEGACY OF COMMON-LAW UNIONS.......................................36

CHAPTER 6: THE INFLUENCE OF AFRICAN HERITAGE 43

CHAPTER 7: THE EXPLOITATION OF ENSLAVED WOMEN 50

CHAPTER 8: THE RISE OF THE NEW FARMERS....57

CHAPTER 9: THE SCATTERING OF FAMILIES THROUGH EMIGRATION 63

CHAPTER 10: THE MOSAIC OF CARIBBEAN IMMIGRATION.......................................70

CHAPTER 11: AFRICAN FAMILIES IN THE CARIBBEAN 77

CHAPTER 12: INDIAN FAMILIES IN THE CARIBBEAN.......................................87

Chapter 13: Chinese Families in the
Caribbean 92

Chapter 14: Jewish Families in the
Caribbean 103

Chapter 15: Conclusion 113

REFERENCES 116

ABOUT THE AUTHOR 119

RECOMMENDED BOOKS 121

ACKNOWLEDGMENT

Without God, nothing is possible that is or was and is to come. Therefore, I am eternally grateful for his gifts, blessings, guidance, and strength. Also, to my biggest supporter, my twin. You are the oil in my engine, the fire in my heart, the meaning for everything, and the answer to why. I thank you for your encouragement, patience, counsel, and your prayers.

-   **Minister Denise N. Fyffe**.

Chapter 1:

Introduction

Being from the Caribbean, I can speak to the reality of family life in our region. I grew up in a nuclear family with two parents, but everything changed when I became a teenager and my mother became the head of the household. This is commonplace in Jamaica and across many Caribbean islands, and although it feels normal to us, it should not be. Almost immediately, our lifestyle shifted. We moved from a multi-room home where extended family lived together, to a shared house with three households under one roof. We shared a kitchen and bathroom and even needed another tenant to help cover the rent.

Soon after, things became even more difficult. I was pursuing tertiary education, and my mother was working around the clock—twenty-four hours a day, five to seven days a week. We moved from a residential neighborhood to progressively lower-income, crime-ridden communities, and eventually into what many would call a "ghetto." This is the reality for countless families across the Caribbean—Jamaica, Trinidad, Haiti, Barbados, the Dominican Republic, St. Lucia, Curaçao, Guyana, Puerto Rico, and more—where matrifocal households depend on one income and carry the weight of poverty, instability, and survival.

Throughout my life, I lived in more than twenty different homes. Without realizing it, I developed a nomadic part of my personality. The breaking of parental ties with my father also shaped my relationships with men. My relationship with him grew distant, and even as a young adult, I could not understand why. This confusion is familiar to many Caribbean women. It is a quiet, unspoken ache that sits beneath the surface while we push through daily life just to keep our heads above water.

These are the effects of broken families. These are the consequences of poverty. These are the patterns we inherit without ever asking for them.

But the answers — and the tools to rebuild — lie in our history. To understand the Caribbean family, we must understand the Afro-Caribbean experience, the legacy of slavery, the psychology of survival, and the cultural influences that shaped each island. Whether English-speaking, Spanish-speaking, French-speaking, or Dutch-speaking, our family structures were formed through a mix of African heritage, colonial systems, migration, indentureship, and economic hardship.

Single-parent homes across the region face cultural, social, financial, and psychological disadvantages. Children often carry adult responsibilities too early. Many leave school to support the family. Crime, unemployment, and instability affect mothers' ability to provide. The eldest child is usually expected to sacrifice so the younger ones can eat or finish primary school — responsibilities that should have been shared by both parents.

Growing up in a single-parent home robs a child of the full benefits a two-parent household can offer. The absence of a father places additional pressure on mothers, affects young girls' future relationships, and leaves young boys without an example of how to be a husband or father. This is one of the reasons single-parent households are so widespread in the Caribbean. Children grow up seeing fathers absent, and that absence becomes a pattern passed down through generations. This pattern was not accidental. It was engineered.

The Willie Lynch ideology left a deep imprint on the Caribbean family. His methods were designed to break the Black family, destroy unity, and create division that would last for centuries.

More than 300 years later, we still see the effects in our homes, relationships, and communities.

Yet, despite all of this, the Caribbean family remains strong, adaptable, and resilient. Across our islands—Jamaica, Trinidad and Tobago, Haiti, Barbados, St. Vincent, Grenada, the Dominican Republic, Martinique, Guadeloupe, Curaçao, Aruba, Suriname, and beyond—our families continue to evolve. We carry the scars of our past, but we also carry the strength of our ancestors.

This book explores the Caribbean family in all its forms: nuclear, matrifocal, extended, blended, common-law, visiting unions, and more. It blends research with lived experience, history with culture, and truth with hope. My prayer is that as you read, you will gain understanding, healing, and a deeper appreciation for the complexity and beauty of our Caribbean families.

Chapter 2:
The Family

The family is the genesis of every society. It is our first classroom, our first government, our first economy, and our first community. Before we ever step into a school or workplace, we learn the meaning of love, authority, responsibility, and belonging within the walls of our home. Whether in Jamaica, Trinidad and Tobago, Haiti, the Dominican Republic, Barbados, Curaçao, St. Lucia, Puerto Rico, or Suriname, the family remains the foundation on which every Caribbean nation stands.

It is within the family that children first learn the value of work, the worth of their possessions, and the importance of cooperation. It is where they experience discipline, compassion, and guidance. Families teach us how to relate to others, how to resolve conflict, and how to navigate the world. They provide the nurturing, protection, and emotional grounding that shape who we become. Even when families are imperfect or strained, they still serve as the first environment where identity is formed and character is shaped.

Every society depends on its families. Without strong families, communities weaken. Without stable homes, nations struggle. As Mehrotra (2005) notes, the family is the most basic social unit, and its structure influences the development of every individual within it. Across the Caribbean — English-speaking, Spanish-speaking, French-speaking, and Dutch-speaking — families differ in form, but their purpose remains the same: to raise, guide, and prepare the next generation.

What Is a Family?

Mehrotra describes the family as a unit that traditionally includes a mother, father, children, and sometimes grandparents or extended relatives. In many Caribbean cultures, roles have historically been defined by gender: men as providers, women as nurturers. While these roles have evolved over time, especially with migration, economic pressures, and changing social norms, the core function of the family remains unchanged.

In the English-speaking Caribbean, families often reflect a blend of African heritage and colonial influence. In the Spanish-speaking Caribbean, such as the Dominican Republic and Puerto Rico, Catholic traditions and extended kinship networks shape family life. In Haiti and Martinique, French and African influences merge, creating strong community-based family structures. In the Dutch-speaking Caribbean—Curaçao, Aruba, and Suriname—families reflect a mix of African, European, and Indigenous traditions. Each island carries its own history, yet all share the belief that family is central to survival and identity.

Functions of the Family

Although families across the Caribbean vary in structure—from nuclear households in Barbados, to matrifocal homes in Jamaica, to extended families in Haiti, to blended families in Trinidad—they all share similar responsibilities. Stewart (2005) identifies the key functions of the family as:

- **Procreation:** ensuring the continuation of the human race.

- **Socialization:** teaching children values, beliefs, religion, culture, and social behavior.

- **Provision:** supplying food, shelter, clothing, healthcare, and love.

- **Cultural transmission:** passing down language, traditions, attitudes, and shared history.

- **Regulating kinship:** preventing incest and defining family boundaries.

- **Conferring status:** giving individuals identity, belonging, and social position.

Across the Caribbean, these functions are carried out in different ways depending on the island's history, culture, and economic realities. In Haiti, extended families often share responsibilities across generations. In the Dominican Republic, migration patterns shape family roles, with many households depending on remittances from relatives abroad. In Trinidad and Guyana, Indian and African traditions influence household structure, shaping expectations around marriage, gender roles, and child-rearing. In Aruba and Curaçao, Dutch cultural norms blend with Afro-Caribbean heritage, creating unique family dynamics.

Yet despite these differences, one truth remains constant: **The family is the heart of Caribbean life.**

It shapes our values, our identity, and our future. It influences our relationships, our choices, and our resilience. It is the first place we learn who we are—and who we can become.

The Family as a Social Anchor

In many Caribbean communities, the family is more than a private unit—it is a social anchor. It provides emotional support, economic stability, and a sense of belonging. Even when families face hardship, they often find creative ways to survive. Grandmothers raise grandchildren while parents migrate for work. Older siblings take on adult responsibilities. Cousins grow up like siblings. Neighbors become extended family. This interconnectedness is one of the defining features of Caribbean life.

In rural Haiti, for example, families often share land, labor, and childcare. In the Dominican Republic, godparents play an important role in guiding children. In Jamaica, "aunties" and "uncles" may not be blood relatives but serve as trusted adults in a child's life. In Trinidad, extended families gather for religious and cultural celebrations that reinforce unity and identity. These practices reflect the communal nature of Caribbean societies.

The Family as a Cultural Bridge

Families also serve as cultural bridges, passing down traditions, languages, and values from one generation to the next. Whether it is Haitian Creole, Jamaican Patois, Dominican Spanish, or Papiamento, language is often learned first at home. Music, food, religious practices, and storytelling are also transmitted through family life. These cultural elements help children understand who they are and where they come from.

Even in families affected by migration, culture remains a powerful connector. Caribbean parents living abroad often work hard to ensure their children maintain ties to their heritage. They teach them the foods, the music, the values, and the stories of home. This cultural continuity strengthens identity and fosters pride.

The Family as a Place of Healing

Finally, the family is a place of healing. Caribbean families have endured centuries of hardship—slavery, colonization, poverty, migration, and social instability. Yet they continue to rise. They continue to adapt. They continue to love. The resilience of the Caribbean family is one of our region's greatest strengths.

Even when families are broken or strained, there is always the possibility of restoration. With understanding, support, and intentional effort, families can heal generational wounds and build healthier futures.

Chapter 3:

Types of Caribbean Families

Families across the Caribbean appear in many shapes and structures. Just as the family has distinct functions, it also exists in diverse forms that reflect the lived experiences of our people. Across the world, seven basic types of families are commonly recognized, and all of them appear throughout the Caribbean—sometimes in traditional ways, sometimes in forms unique to our region.

Global Family Forms

The seven basic family forms found worldwide include:

- **Nuclear:** parents and one or more children.

- **Single Parent**: one parent raising a child or children.

- **Extended**: a nuclear or single-parent family living with extended relatives.

- **Blended**: a family in which one or both parents have children from previous unions.

- **Adoptive**: any family form where the child is legally adopted.

- **Foster**: any family form where a child is placed through government or private agencies.

- **Other types:** households that do not include parents and children, such as newly married couples or communal living arrangements.

These forms exist across English, Spanish, French, and Dutch speaking Caribbean islands. However, the Caribbean has also developed its own variations, shaped by slavery, indentureship, migration, poverty, and cultural traditions.

Caribbean Family Forms

The Family Code of the Caribbean reminds us that "the family is the elementary cell of society," responsible for nurturing, socializing, and preparing the next generation. In our region, the following family forms are especially prominent.

First let's discuss the nuclear family. It consists of two married, heterosexual parents and their biological or legally recognized children. Mehrotra notes that this is the most conventional form in the Western hemisphere. In the Caribbean, nuclear families are common in Barbados, Trinidad and Tobago, the Dominican Republic, Puerto Rico, and parts of the Dutch Caribbean. However, the nuclear family has evolved. Economic pressures, migration, and shifting gender roles have reshaped the traditional model. Two forms once considered "unconventional" are now widespread:

- Single-parent families headed by women
- Families formed through de facto (common-law) unions

These changes reflect the social and economic realities of Caribbean life.

Now the matrifocal family, which is headed by a mother, is one of the most dominant family forms in the Caribbean. This form has deep historical roots and remains widespread today across Jamaica, Barbados, Trinidad and Tobago, Antigua, Grenada, St. Lucia, Haiti, and parts of the Dutch Caribbean. While exact percentages vary by island, the overall trend is clear: female-headed households remain one of the most common family structures in the region, and their numbers have continued to rise over the past two decades.

Several factors contribute to this pattern:

- migration for work
- economic instability
- relationship breakdown
- cultural norms rooted in our history
- fathers who are present emotionally but not physically

- fathers who contribute financially but do not reside in the home

In many Caribbean homes, mothers are the backbone of the family. They work multiple jobs, manage the household, and raise children with limited support. This is not simply a statistic — it is a lived reality for thousands of women across the region.

Another type of family formed in the Caribbean are common-law (de facto) unions. These remain widespread across the Caribbean. In many islands, these unions are just as stable and committed as legal marriages. Couples live together, raise children, and build lives without formalizing the relationship through the state. This form of family life continues to grow, especially among younger couples and those facing economic challenges. Marriage is expensive, and for many families, love, commitment, and shared responsibility matter more than a legal certificate.

In Jamaica, the law still recognizes long-term cohabiting partners under the Property (Rights of Spouses) Act, giving them access to maintenance and shared property rights after five years of living together. Other islands have similar protections, while some still rely on traditional norms. Across the region — from Trinidad to Haiti, from the Dominican Republic to Curaçao — common-law unions reflect the flexibility and adaptability of Caribbean families.

Extended or consanguineal families remain one of the strongest and most culturally rooted forms of family life in the Caribbean. This form is especially common in Haiti, Dominica, St. Lucia, rural Guyana, and low-income communities across the region.

Extended families continue to serve as childcare networks, emotional support systems, economic safety nets and cultural anchors. Grandmothers, aunties, cousins, and even close neighbors often step in to help raise children. This is not a sign of weakness, it is a sign of community. It reflects the African heritage of collective child-rearing and the Caribbean tradition of "each one help one." Even with modernization, migration, and changing social norms, extended families remain essential to the survival and stability of many households.

Then there are visiting unions, which continue to be a unique and very real part of Caribbean family life. These relationships are especially common among younger couples, those still living with their parents, or individuals who are not yet ready — or financially able — to establish a shared household. In a visiting union, partners live separately. They meet at agreed times and the relationship may be romantic, sexual, or social. Children usually reside with the mother and the father may contribute financially or emotionally, depending on the situation.

This form of union remains prevalent in Jamaica, St. Vincent, Grenada, Haiti, and parts of the Spanish-speaking Caribbean. It is often a transitional stage that may evolve into a common-law union or a nuclear family. The important thing is this: visiting unions are not casual or irresponsible by default. They are shaped by economic realities, cultural norms, and the lived experiences of Caribbean people.

The Fluidity of Caribbean Family Forms

Professor Barry Chevannes observed that "families are like human organisms; they live, and they die." Family forms are transitional and may shift over time due to death, migration, economic hardship and/or relationship changes. A family may move from a visiting union to a nuclear family, then to marriage, then to an extended household. These cycles can occur in any order, reflecting the fluid and adaptive nature of Caribbean family life.

Chapter 4:
The Impact of Slavery

The story of the Caribbean family cannot be understood without returning to the brutal foundation on which our societies were built. Slavery was not only an economic system; it was a deliberate and calculated assault on the African person, the African spirit, and the African family. It disrupted every structure that held communities together. It stripped men, women, and children of their names, their languages, their kinship systems, and their sense of belonging. And although centuries have passed, the imprint of that destruction still shapes the families we see across the Caribbean today.

Frazier once argued that enslavement destroyed African culture so thoroughly that only faint memories remained. Barrow described how, at every stage of the journey—from capture to the Middle Passage, to the plantations—enslaved Africans were systematically stripped of their customs, their identities, and their family structures. What survived had to survive in fragments, carried in songs, in whispered stories, in spiritual practices, and in the quiet resilience of a people determined not to disappear.

Across Jamaica, Barbados, Trinidad, Haiti, the Dominican Republic, Martinique, Guadeloupe, Curaçao, Suriname, and the wider Caribbean, Africans were uprooted from diverse ethnic groups and kinship systems. They came from societies where family was sacred, where lineage was honored, and where community was central to identity. But on the plantations, these systems were intentionally dismantled.

The slave owners understood something powerful: if you break the family, you break the people. And so they attacked the family first. Men, women, and children were separated and sold to different plantations. A mother could be sent to one island, her child to another. A father could be sold away without warning. Many families never saw each other again.

This was not accidental; it was strategic. The goal was to weaken unity, destroy resistance, and create dependency on the plantation system. The enslaved were denied the right to marry, denied the right to raise their children, and denied the right to maintain family bonds. The nuclear family — mother, father, and children — was nearly impossible to sustain under such conditions.

The Willie Lynch ideology played a significant role in shaping the psychological and social landscape of the Caribbean family. Whether or not every detail of the speech is historically verified, the methods it describes were undeniably practiced. The strategy was to divide the enslaved, pit them against each other, destroy trust, break the male figure, elevate the mother as the sole stabilizing force, and create generational patterns of fear, dependency, and fragmentation. These methods were designed to last for centuries, and in many ways, they did.

During slavery, the responsibility of raising children rested primarily with mothers and grandmothers. Fathers were often absent, not because they chose to be, but because they were forcibly removed. This gave rise to the matrifocal household, a structure that remains deeply rooted in Caribbean society today. In many islands, from Jamaica to Haiti, from Barbados to Trinidad, and across the Dutch Caribbean, households led by women continue to be one of the most common family forms. This is not because Caribbean women are unwilling to share responsibility, but because history placed the weight of family survival on their shoulders. The matrifocal household is not a sign of failure; it is a sign of resilience. It is evidence of the strength of Caribbean women who held their families together when everything around them was designed to tear them apart.

The plantation system also distorted ideas of marriage, partnership, and intimacy. Enslaved people were not allowed to marry legally. Their unions were not recognized or protected. Couples could be separated at any moment. Children could be taken away and sold. This instability created patterns that continued long after emancipation. Relationships formed without legal marriage. Unions were shaped by proximity rather than long-term security. Fathers were often emotionally present but physically absent. Mothers carried the full responsibility of raising children. Extended families stepped in to support child-rearing. These patterns were not cultural flaws; they were survival strategies.

As African customs were suppressed, enslaved people were pressured to adopt the beliefs and practices of the plantation owners. Frazier noted that enslaved Africans often took on the attitudes of their masters toward religion, sex, and marriage. This was not a willing adoption; it was forced assimilation. Yet, even in this cultural vacuum, African identity survived. It survived in the rhythms of our music, in the flavors of our food, in the strength of our women, in the resilience of our men, in the communal nature of our families, and in the spirituality that carried us through suffering. The Caribbean family today is a blend of African heritage, colonial influence, and the lived experiences of generations who refused to be erased.

Slavery ended on paper, but its effects did not disappear. They show up in the high number of female-headed households, in the challenges many men face in embracing fatherhood, in the mistrust that sometimes shadows long-term relationships, in the economic instability that affects family life, and in the emotional wounds passed down through generations. But they also show up in our strength. They show up in our ability to adapt, in our deep sense of community, in our commitment to children, in our cultural pride, in our spiritual resilience, and in our determination to rise.

The Caribbean family is not broken. It is battle-tested. It is not weak. It is survivor-strong. It is not lost. It is still healing. Understanding slavery is not about dwelling on the past. It is about recognizing the roots of our present so we can build healthier, stronger families for the future.

Chapter 5:

The Legacy of Common-Law Unions

When we speak about the Caribbean family, we must speak honestly about the forms of union that have shaped our region for generations. One of the most enduring and misunderstood of these is the common-law union, sometimes called faithful concubinage. It is a form of partnership that grew out of our history, our struggles, and the realities of life in societies shaped by slavery, colonization, and economic hardship. To understand it, we must look beyond judgment and see the human stories, the cultural patterns, and the survival instincts that gave rise to it.

During slavery, enslaved Africans were denied the right to marry legally. Their unions were not recognized, protected, or respected. Couples could be separated at any moment, and children could be taken away without warning. Under such conditions, the idea of a stable, legally sanctioned marriage was almost impossible. Yet people still formed bonds. They still sought companionship, intimacy, and family. They still tried to build something resembling a home, even when the system around them refused to acknowledge it. These early unions were not legal, but they were deeply human. They were acts of resistance, of hope, and of survival.

After emancipation, the legacy of these non-legal unions continued. Many formerly enslaved people had no land, no resources, and no legal standing. Marriage required fees, documentation, and church approval—things that were out of reach for the poor. And so, the practice of forming unions without legal marriage persisted. Over time, it became woven into the cultural fabric of the Caribbean. In many communities, a couple living together, raising children, and sharing responsibilities was considered just as legitimate as a married couple. Their commitment was measured not by a certificate, but by their daily life together.

In Jamaica, Trinidad, Haiti, the Dominican Republic, and across the Dutch Caribbean, common-law unions became a normal part of family life. They were not seen as lesser or inferior. They were simply another way families were formed. In some communities, these unions were even preferred, because they allowed couples to build trust and stability before formalizing their relationship. In others, economic hardship made legal marriage unrealistic. And in many cases, couples remained together faithfully for decades without ever stepping into a courthouse or church.

The term "faithful concubinage" may sound outdated today, but it reflects a historical reality. In earlier centuries, it described long-term, committed relationships that existed outside the institution of marriage. These unions were often stable, loving, and enduring. They produced children, built households, and created family lines that continue today. Yet they were not recognized by the law, and the women in these unions often had no legal protection if the relationship ended or if the man died.

Over time, Caribbean societies began to acknowledge the legitimacy of these unions. In Jamaica, for example, the Property (Rights of Spouses) Act recognizes long-term cohabiting partners and grants them rights similar to those of legally married spouses. This shift reflects a deeper truth: common-law unions are not a sign of moral failure or cultural deficiency. They reflect our history, our resilience, and our ability to create family even in the face of hardship.

In many Caribbean households, common-law unions function with the same level of commitment, love, and responsibility as legal marriages. Couples share finances, raise children, support each other through illness, and build homes together. Their relationships are often rooted in mutual respect and shared struggle. For many, the absence of a legal certificate does not diminish the depth of their bond.

At the same time, we must acknowledge the challenges that come with this form of union. Without legal recognition, women — especially those who have sacrificed years of their lives to a relationship — may find themselves vulnerable if the union ends. Children may face complications with inheritance. Property disputes can become painful and prolonged. These challenges are not unique to the Caribbean, but they are more pronounced in societies where common-law unions are widespread.

Yet even with these challenges, common-law unions remain a central part of Caribbean family life. They reflect the flexibility and adaptability of our people. They show how families can form and thrive even when systems fail to support them. They remind us that love and commitment do not always follow the paths laid out by law or tradition.

In pastoral work, I have met many couples who have lived together faithfully for decades without ever marrying. Some never felt the need. Others planned to marry but were hindered by finances, migration, or family obligations. Some simply believed that their commitment to each other was enough. And in many cases, it was. Their homes were filled with love, stability, and mutual respect. Their children grew up in environments where they were cared for, guided, and supported. These families were no less real, no less valid, and no less meaningful than those formed through legal marriage.

As we look at the Caribbean family today, we must approach common-law unions with understanding and compassion. We must see them not as deviations from an ideal, but as expressions of resilience in a region shaped by hardship. We must recognize the historical forces that made legal marriage inaccessible for so many. And we must honor the families that were built in spite of those barriers.

The Caribbean family is diverse, complex, and deeply rooted in survival. Common-law unions are part of that story. They remind us that love finds a way, even when systems fail. They show us that families can be strong, stable, and nurturing, even without legal recognition. And they challenge us to look beyond labels and see the heart of what truly makes a family: commitment, care, and the courage to build a life together.

Chapter 6:

The Influence of African Heritage

When we look at the Caribbean family today, we cannot separate who we are from where we came from. Long before the ships crossed the Atlantic, long before the plantations and the brutality of slavery, African societies had their own rich, complex, and deeply rooted family systems. These systems shaped how people loved, how they partnered, how they raised children, and how they built community. Even though slavery attempted to erase these traditions, traces of them survived — sometimes in obvious ways, sometimes in quiet, subtle patterns that still show up in our families today.

Most of the Africans brought to the Caribbean came from West Africa, a region with diverse ethnic groups and cultural practices. Among many of these groups, polygamy was a normal and respected part of family life. A man might have several wives, and each wife had her own space within a shared compound. These were not chaotic or unstable arrangements; they were structured, communal, and rooted in cultural norms that valued lineage, fertility, and the continuity of the family line. Children grew up surrounded by siblings, cousins, aunties, and co-wives who all played a role in their upbringing. Family was not a small, isolated unit—it was a living community.

In some African societies, a man's virility was measured by the number of children he fathered, especially sons. Chiefs and leaders were often chosen based on their physical strength, their ability to protect the community, and their capacity to produce many offspring. Fertility was not simply a personal matter; it was tied to status, legacy, and the survival of the tribe. Stewart

(2005) notes that this emphasis on virility and offspring was deeply embedded in many West African cultures. When we look at the Caribbean today, it is not surprising that echoes of this mindset remain. It is still common to hear men boast about the number of children they have, as if it is a sign of strength or masculinity. This is not a modern invention—it is a cultural memory, carried across the ocean and reshaped by centuries of history.

When enslaved Africans arrived in the Caribbean, they brought these cultural patterns with them. But the plantation system did not allow these traditions to flourish in their original form. Polygamy, lineage, and communal child-rearing were disrupted by the violence of slavery. Families were torn apart. Men were separated from women. Children were sold away. The extended family networks that once supported African households were replaced by the harsh reality of plantation life. Yet even in this environment, African cultural values found ways to survive.

One of the most enduring legacies of African heritage is the communal approach to raising children. In many Caribbean communities today—whether in Jamaica, Haiti, Trinidad, Barbados, St. Lucia, or Suriname—it is normal for children to be cared for by grandparents, aunties, cousins, godparents, and even close family friends. This is not simply a response to hardship; it is a continuation of an African worldview that sees child-rearing as a shared responsibility. The idea that "it takes a village to raise a child" is not a cliché for us—it is a lived reality rooted in our ancestral past.

Another legacy is the fluidity of family structures. In West Africa, family was not defined solely by a mother, father, and children. It included extended kin, lineage groups, and community ties. When slavery disrupted the nuclear family, Caribbean people adapted by forming new family networks that resembled the communal systems of their ancestors. Even today, many Caribbean families do not fit neatly into Western definitions. We have blended families, visiting unions, common-law partnerships, and extended households that reflect both our history and our cultural flexibility.

African heritage also influenced gender roles within the family. In many West African societies, women held significant authority within the household. They managed resources, raised children, and maintained the social fabric of the community. When slavery forced men into physical separation or economic instability, Caribbean women stepped into leadership roles within the home. This was not new to them—it was an extension of the strength and responsibility African women had always carried. The matrifocal household, so common in the Caribbean today, is not only a product of slavery; it is also a reflection of African traditions where women were central to family life.

At the same time, the African emphasis on male virility and fatherhood did not disappear. It simply took on new forms. In some communities, a man's identity is still tied to his ability to father children, even if he does not live with them. This pattern is often misunderstood as irresponsibility, but its roots are cultural, not merely behavioral. It reflects a worldview where fatherhood is connected to lineage and legacy, even when the structure of the household is different from Western norms.

African spirituality also shaped the Caribbean family. The belief in ancestors, the respect for elders, the value placed on community rituals, and the understanding that life is interconnected — all of these continue to influence how Caribbean families function. Even within Christian households, African ways of thinking about family, protection, and spiritual covering remain present. We see it in the way we pray, the way we bless our children, the way we honor our elders, and the way we gather as family during times of crisis.

The African heritage within the Caribbean family is not a relic of the past. It is alive. It is woven into our language, our food, our music, our relationships, and our understanding of what it means to belong. It shows up in the grandmother who raises her grandchildren with fierce love. It shows up in the cousin who becomes a sibling. It shows up in the man who takes pride in his children, even if he does not live in the same home. It shows up in the mother who leads her household with strength and grace. It shows up in the community that steps in when a family is struggling.

To understand the Caribbean family, we must honor the African roots that continue to shape us. These roots remind us that our families are resilient, adaptable, and deeply connected to a history that predates slavery. They remind us that our identity is not defined by the trauma we endured, but by the strength we carried with us. And they remind us that even after centuries of disruption, the spirit of our ancestors still lives in the way we love, the way we raise our children, and the way we build family.

Chapter 7:

The Exploitation of Enslaved Women

The story of the Caribbean family cannot be told without acknowledging the painful and often hidden experiences of enslaved women. Their bodies, their choices, and their futures were not their own. They lived under a system that saw them not as human beings, but as property — objects to be used, traded, and controlled. Yet even in this darkness, they carried a strength that shaped generations. To understand the Caribbean family today, we must honor their truth with honesty, compassion, and reverence.

Enslaved women lived under constant threat. Their days were filled with back-breaking labor, emotional trauma, and the ever-present fear of punishment. But beyond the physical brutality, there was another layer of suffering that history often glosses over: the sexual exploitation they endured at the hands of planters, overseers, and slave masters. This exploitation was not incidental; it was woven into the fabric of the plantation system. Women were targeted because their bodies could produce more enslaved people, increasing the wealth of the plantation owners. Their fertility was seen as an economic asset, not a sacred part of their humanity.

Many enslaved women longed for freedom — not only for themselves, but for their children. They dreamed of a life where their sons and daughters would not be born into chains. They wanted relief from the harshness of field labor, where the sun scorched their backs and the whip threatened their every move. They wanted the dignity of working in the house rather than the fields, where conditions were slightly less brutal. And in the cruel logic of slavery, one of the few ways to gain these small mercies was to submit to the sexual advances of the men who owned them.

This submission was not consent. It was survival.

Stewart (2005) notes that many enslaved women bore children for their masters in hopes of securing better treatment or improving their children's chances of freedom. Some hoped that the father's affection—or guilt—might lead to manumission. Others simply wanted to escape the relentless toil of the fields. These choices were not made freely; they were made under duress, within a system that offered no real alternatives. Their bodies became bargaining tools in a world where they had no power.

The children born from these unions lived complicated lives. Some were given lighter duties or allowed to work in the house. Others were sold away, a constant reminder that even the planter's own blood could be treated as property. The emotional toll on enslaved women was immeasurable. They carried the weight of protecting their children in a world where protection was nearly impossible. They navigated relationships shaped by coercion, fear, and the desperate hope for a better future.

This history left deep marks on the Caribbean family. The imbalance of power between men and women, the vulnerability of women in economic hardship, and the complex dynamics of intimacy under oppression all shaped the patterns we see today. Even though the context has changed, echoes of this exploitation remain. In some parts of the Caribbean, there are still situations where women feel pressured to exchange affection, companionship, or sexual favors for financial support, job opportunities, or social advancement. While the scale is far smaller and the circumstances are different, the underlying dynamic—women navigating power imbalances to survive—has roots in the plantation era.

Yet it is important to say this clearly: Caribbean women are not defined by victimhood. They are defined by resilience. The enslaved women who endured exploitation were not passive. They were strategic, courageous, and determined to carve out whatever dignity they could in a world designed to strip it away. They protected their children fiercely. They formed sisterhoods with other women. They passed down stories, songs, and spiritual practices that kept their identity alive. They resisted in ways both quiet and bold. Their strength is the foundation on which Caribbean womanhood stands today.

The legacy of their suffering is visible, but so is the legacy of their strength. Caribbean women continue to lead households, nurture communities, and carry the emotional weight of family life with grace. They continue to navigate systems that are not always fair, drawing on the same resilience that sustained their ancestors. And Caribbean men, too, are shaped by this history—often without realizing it. The patterns of absence, emotional distance, or fragmented fatherhood that appear in some families are not simply personal failings; they are the long shadows of a system that once denied men the right to protect, provide for, or even remain with their families.

Understanding the sexual exploitation of enslaved women is not about reopening wounds. It is about acknowledging the truth so that healing can continue. It is about recognizing that the Caribbean family did not emerge from a vacuum; it emerged from trauma, survival, and the unbreakable will of a people who refused to be destroyed. When we honor the stories of enslaved women, we honor the roots of our resilience. We honor the mothers who held their families together in impossible circumstances. We honor the women whose strength still flows through our bloodlines.

The Caribbean family is complex, layered, and deeply shaped by history. But it is also beautiful, resilient, and full of hope. The story of enslaved women reminds us that even in the darkest chapters of our past, there were seeds of strength, courage, and endurance. Those seeds grew into the families we see today—families that continue to rise, continue to adapt, and continue to carry the legacy of survival with dignity.

Chapter 8:

The Rise of the New Farmers

When emancipation finally arrived in the Caribbean, freedom did not come with land, money, or opportunity. It came with uncertainty. It came with the weight of survival. Yet it also came with a fierce determination among the formerly enslaved to build a life that was truly their own. One of the most significant shifts during this period was the rise of the "new farmers"—men and women who walked away from the plantations and began carving out small pieces of independence on the land.

Stewart (2005) describes how, after emancipation, many ex-slaves deserted the estates in search of better living conditions and a sense of dignity that plantation life had long denied them. They were no longer willing to live under the watchful eyes of former masters or endure the humiliation of forced labor. Freedom meant distance—distance from the fields where they had been beaten, distance from the overseers who had controlled their every movement, and distance from the trauma that lingered in the soil itself.

With the help of missionaries, many freed people were able to purchase small plots of land—sometimes no more than a few acres. Others squatted on crown lands or on properties owned by absentee landlords. These plots were humble, often rocky or remote, but they represented something priceless: autonomy. For the first time, families could plant what they wanted, work at their own pace, and build homes without fear of being uprooted. The land became a symbol of hope, a quiet declaration that they were no longer property but people with a future.

Missionaries played a complicated but influential role during this period. They encouraged marriage among the freed population, believing that Christian marriage would bring stability and moral order to communities emerging from the chaos of slavery. For many newly freed couples, marriage was not simply a religious act—it was a reclaiming of something they had been denied for generations. It was a way of saying, "We belong to each other, and no one can take this from us." These early marriages helped shape the foundation of the post-emancipation Caribbean family.

Life as a new farmer, however, was far from easy. Many of the plots were located in remote areas, far from markets and trading centers. Roads were poor or nonexistent. Farmers often had to rely on donkeys to transport their produce, or they sold their goods to higglers who carried baskets on their heads and walked miles to reach buyers. The work was demanding, and the income was unpredictable. Yet families persisted because the alternative—returning to plantation labor—was unthinkable.

This new way of life created both opportunities and challenges for families. On one hand, owning land allowed families to work together, build homes, and establish roots. On the other hand, the demands of farming often pulled parents away from their children for long hours. In many households, children were kept from school to help with chores, care for younger siblings, or prepare produce for market. Education became a luxury that many could not afford, not because they did not value it, but because survival required every pair of hands.

The consequences of this were profound. Children who spent their days working instead of learning were often trapped in the same cycle of poverty as their parents. Their dreams were limited by the demands of the land and the absence of opportunity. The burden fell especially hard on the eldest daughters, who were expected to take on adult responsibilities long before they were ready. These patterns shaped the rhythm of family life for generations.

Even today, we see echoes of this dynamic in the phenomenon of "barrel children." Parents migrate to the United States, Canada, the United Kingdom, or other Caribbean islands in search of better wages and a chance to provide for their families. They send home money, clothes, and barrels filled with food and supplies. But the emotional cost is high. Children grow up without the daily presence of their parents. They are raised by grandparents, older siblings, or extended family members who do their best but cannot replace the bond of a mother or father.

Like the children of the new farmers, barrel children often carry responsibilities far beyond their years. They navigate loneliness, confusion, and the ache of separation. Some thrive despite the distance; others struggle with behavioral challenges, academic setbacks, or early exposure to adult situations. The absence of parental supervision can leave them vulnerable, and the longing for connection can shape their choices in ways that echo through adulthood.

The story of the new farmers is not simply a historical footnote. It is a reminder of how deeply economic survival shapes family life. It shows us that the Caribbean family has always been resilient, always adapting, always finding ways to endure despite limited resources. It also reveals the quiet sacrifices made by parents who work tirelessly—whether on a hillside farm or in a foreign country—to give their children a better life.

As we reflect on this chapter of our history, we see both the beauty and the burden of freedom. The new farmers carved out spaces of independence with their bare hands. They built homes where none existed. They planted seeds in soil that had once been a place of suffering. And they raised families with a determination that still inspires us today. Their story is a testament to the courage it takes to begin again, to build from nothing, and to believe that the future can be better than the past.

Chapter 9:

The Scattering of Families Through Emigration

The Caribbean has always been a region on the move. Long before modern airports and visa lines, our people were crossing waters in search of survival, opportunity, and dignity. Emigration is woven into the fabric of our history, shaping not only our economies but the very structure of our families. To understand the Caribbean home today, we must understand the journeys—both voluntary and forced—that pulled families apart and reshaped the meaning of belonging.

After emancipation, the Caribbean entered a new era of mobility. The plantation system no longer held people in place, but poverty, limited opportunities, and the lure of better wages elsewhere pushed them outward. By the late nineteenth and early twentieth centuries, thousands of Jamaicans were leaving for Cuba, Panama, Costa Rica, and the United States. They went to cut cane, dig canals, build railroads, and take on the hardest labor available. Many of these migrants were fathers who left with the hope of sending money home, believing that temporary separation would lead to long-term stability. But temporary often became permanent. Letters slowed, money stopped, and families were left to rebuild themselves around the absence.

In the 1950s, another wave of migration swept through the region. Jamaicans boarded ships bound for England, joining the Windrush generation that helped rebuild Britain after the war. This time, it was not only fathers who left — mothers, too, sought better wages and a chance to lift their families out of poverty. Children were left in the care of grandmothers, aunties, older siblings, or trusted neighbors. These caregivers did their best, but nothing could replace the daily presence of a parent. Many children grew up with a sense of longing, waiting for a mother they barely remembered or a father they knew only through stories.

This pattern was not unique to Jamaica. Across Guyana, Trinidad, Barbados, St. Lucia, Haiti, and the Dutch Caribbean, migration became a defining feature of family life. In Guyana, the National Development Strategy noted that in some Amerindian communities, fathers were absent for long stretches due to work in mining and logging camps deep in the hinterland. These men were not abandoning their families; they were trying to provide. But their absence created households where mothers carried the full emotional and financial weight, and children grew up navigating the silence left behind.

Migration affects families differently depending on class and resources. Wealthier families may migrate together, maintaining their household structure even in a new country. But for poor families, migration often happens one person at a time. A mother leaves first, then a father, then perhaps an older sibling. The family becomes stretched across borders, held together by phone calls, remittances, and the hope of reunion. But distance has a way of changing relationships. Children grow up. Parents build new lives abroad. The dream of returning home fades. And the family that once existed in one place becomes scattered across continents.

This scattering has consequences. When adults migrate alone, children are often left to navigate life with limited supervision. Some thrive under the care of extended family, but others struggle with feelings of abandonment, confusion, or resentment. The term "child-shifting" emerged to describe the movement of children from one caregiver to another as parents migrate. In some cases, children end up in households where they are treated differently from biological children, receiving less affection, fewer resources, or harsher discipline. These experiences shape their sense of self and their understanding of family.

A study conducted in Georgetown, Guyana, revealed the emotional toll of parental migration. Many children reported negative expectations about reuniting with their parents, unsure of how to rebuild relationships after years of separation. Some families had broken apart permanently, unable to withstand the strain of distance. Others struggled to reconnect, discovering that love alone could not bridge the gap created by time and absence. These stories are not isolated—they reflect a regional reality that continues today.

Modern migration has created a new kind of Caribbean family: one that exists across borders, held together by technology, remittances, and the hope of a better future. Parents abroad work long hours, often in jobs below their qualifications, sending money home to pay school fees, build houses, or support elderly relatives. Their sacrifice is real, but so is the emotional cost. Children grow up with material stability but emotional distance. Parents carry guilt, longing, and the pressure to justify their absence through financial support. The heart of the family stretches thin, trying to remain whole across oceans.

Yet, even in this complexity, there is resilience. Caribbean families have learned to adapt, to maintain connection through voice notes, video calls, and holiday reunions. Grandmothers step into the role of mother with grace. Older siblings become protectors and guides. Communities rally around children who need support. The story of emigration is not only one of loss—it is also one of endurance, sacrifice, and the unbreakable desire to create a better life for the next generation.

As we reflect on this chapter of our history, we see how movement has shaped us. Emigration has pulled families apart, but it has also opened doors. It has created new opportunities, new identities, and new ways of belonging. It has challenged us to redefine what family means when love must travel across borders. And it has shown us that even when separated by oceans, the bonds of family can remain strong—if nurtured with intention, honesty, and grace.

Chapter 10:

The Mosaic of Caribbean Immigration

The Caribbean is a place shaped not only by those who were brought here by force, but also by those who arrived seeking opportunity, refuge, or a new beginning. Immigration has been one of the most powerful forces in shaping the diversity of Caribbean families. Long after the arrival of enslaved Africans, new groups came from India, China, the Middle East, and Europe, each carrying their own traditions, beliefs, and family structures. Their presence added new layers to the cultural landscape, creating a region where difference became part of the identity itself.

When indentureship began in the nineteenth century, thousands of Indians and Chinese journeyed across the seas to the Caribbean. They came under contracts that promised work, wages, and the possibility of a better life. Many arrived with little more than hope and the memory of the families they left behind. They stepped into societies still reeling from the trauma of slavery, and their arrival introduced new customs, new languages, and new ways of forming family. Over time, these groups established communities, built businesses, and raised children who would become part of the Caribbean story.

Indian families brought with them strong kinship networks, arranged marriage traditions, and a deep sense of cultural continuity. Their households were often multigenerational, with grandparents, parents, and children living under one roof. Marriage was not simply a union between two individuals but a joining of families. Religion, ritual, and ancestral memory shaped their daily lives. Even today, in places like Trinidad, Guyana, and Suriname, the influence of Indian family structures remains visible in the emphasis on extended kin, respect for elders, and the preservation of cultural practices across generations.

Chinese immigrants also left a lasting imprint on the Caribbean family. Many arrived as indentured laborers, but over time they became known for their entrepreneurial spirit. They opened shops, built businesses, and created tight-knit communities that valued discipline, education, and family loyalty. Their households often blended traditional Chinese values with the realities of Caribbean life, producing families that were both culturally distinct and deeply integrated into the wider society. The Chinese presence, though smaller in number, contributed significantly to the economic and cultural fabric of islands like Jamaica, Trinidad, and Guyana.

Middle Eastern families—particularly those from Lebanon and Syria—arrived later, often as merchants seeking new markets. They, too, brought strong family traditions, emphasizing unity, hard work, and the importance of maintaining cultural identity. Their children grew up navigating the balance between preserving their heritage and embracing the rhythms of Caribbean life. Over time, many of these families became pillars of commerce and community leadership.

European immigrants, though fewer in number after the colonial period, also contributed to the diversity of the region. Some came as teachers, missionaries, or professionals. Others arrived seeking opportunity in the growing economies of the twentieth century. Their presence added yet another layer to the cultural mosaic, influencing education, religion, and social structures.

By the time Jamaica gained independence in 1962, the island had become a tapestry of cultures. The framers of the constitution recognized this reality when they chose the motto "Out of Many, One People." It was not a slogan—it was a truth. The Caribbean had become a place where African, Indian, Chinese, Middle Eastern, and European families lived side by side, each contributing to the shared identity of the nation. This diversity did not erase the wounds of the past, but it offered a vision of unity that transcended race, ethnicity, and origin.

Immigration reshaped the Caribbean family in profound ways. It introduced new marriage customs, new parenting styles, and new expectations around gender roles. It brought different religious traditions—Hinduism, Islam, Buddhism, Christianity—and allowed them to coexist in a region already rich with African spirituality. It created communities where a child might grow up eating roti, jerk chicken, chow mein, and pelau, all within the same neighborhood. It fostered friendships, marriages, and blended families that reflected the region's evolving identity.

But immigration also brought challenges. Cultural differences sometimes created tension. Communities struggled to understand one another's customs, and prejudices emerged on all sides. Yet, over time, the shared experience of living in the Caribbean—of facing the same storms, celebrating the same festivals, and navigating the same economic realities—created a sense of belonging that transcended origin. The region became a living example of how diversity can coexist with unity.

Today, the Caribbean continues to be shaped by immigration. New waves of migrants arrive from Latin America, Asia, and Africa, adding fresh threads to the tapestry. Their presence reminds us that the Caribbean is not static—it is a place of movement, exchange, and transformation. The families they form, the traditions they bring, and the communities they build will shape the next chapter of our regional identity.

Immigration has taught us that family is not defined by sameness but by connection. It has shown us that a nation can be strengthened, not weakened, by diversity. And it has given the Caribbean a unique gift: the ability to hold many cultures within one shared home, each contributing to the richness of who we are.

Chapter 11:

African Families in the Caribbean

African families form the heartbeat of the Caribbean. Their presence is not a footnote in our history but the foundation on which much of our culture, identity, and social life has been built. When Africans were brought to the Caribbean between the seventeenth and nineteenth centuries, they carried with them languages, customs, spiritual practices, and family structures that would eventually shape the region in profound ways. Even though slavery attempted to dismantle these traditions, the essence of African family life survived—sometimes in fragments, sometimes in full expression—and continues to influence Caribbean families today.

The majority of enslaved Africans brought to the Caribbean came from West Africa, particularly from Akan and Igbo communities. The Akan people, originating from present-day Ghana and Ivory Coast, carried with them a strong sense of matrilineal identity, communal responsibility, and spiritual depth. The Igbo, from Nigeria and surrounding regions, brought traditions rooted in kinship, resilience, and a deep respect for personal agency. These cultural foundations did not disappear on the plantations; they adapted, merged, and re-emerged in new forms that still echo through Caribbean households.

One of the most remarkable expressions of African resilience in the Caribbean is found in the Maroon communities. These were Africans who refused to remain enslaved. They fought alongside the Spaniards against the British, and when the tides of power shifted, they retreated into the mountains of Jamaica, creating independent settlements far from the reach of plantation owners. The terrain was rugged and unforgiving, but it offered freedom. In places like Accompong, these communities preserved African customs, governance structures, and family patterns with a purity that is still visible today. Their survival is a testament to the determination of African families to protect their identity at all costs.

Across the Caribbean, African families became the majority population. In many islands, they make up more than eighty percent of households, shaping everything from language to food to spirituality. Even in places like Trinidad and Guyana, where the African population is closer to half, the influence of African culture remains unmistakable. The rhythms of daily life—how we raise children, how we gather as family, how we celebrate, how we mourn—carry the imprint of African heritage.

African families in the Caribbean have always been diverse. Some traditions reflect matrilineal structures, where women hold central authority in the home. Others reflect patrilineal customs, where lineage and inheritance pass through the father's line. But across these variations, one theme remains constant: family is not limited to the nuclear unit. It extends outward to aunties, uncles, cousins, godparents, neighbors, and community elders. This expansive understanding of family is deeply African, rooted in the belief that raising a child is a communal responsibility and that belonging is not confined to bloodlines alone.

The cultural contributions of African families are woven into every corner of Caribbean life. Our music—whether Mento, Kumina, Junkanoo, Rock Steady, Ska, Calypso, Dancehall, or Reggae—carries African rhythms, call-and-response patterns, and spiritual undertones. Carnival celebrations, with their vibrant colors and expressive movement, echo African festivals that honored ancestors, harvests, and community unity. Even the steel pan, born in Trinidad, carries the improvisational spirit and creative resilience that African families nurtured through generations of hardship and hope.

African influence is also visible in the values that shape Caribbean households. Respect for elders remains a cornerstone of family life. Storytelling continues to be a way of passing down wisdom, history, and moral lessons. Spirituality—whether expressed through Christianity, Revivalism, Rastafari, or ancestral practices—remains central to how families understand themselves and their place in the world. These values did not emerge by accident; they were carried across the Atlantic, preserved through suffering, and passed down with intention.

The strength of African families is reflected in the remarkable individuals who have emerged from this heritage. Jamaica alone has produced cultural icons, freedom fighters, athletes, musicians, and thinkers whose influence has reached every corner of the globe. Their achievements are not isolated successes; they are the fruit of communities that nurtured talent, resilience, and creativity despite limited resources. They stand as reminders that African families in the Caribbean have always been builders — of culture, of identity, of legacy.

Yet the story of African families is not only one of triumph. It is also a story of adaptation. The disruptions of slavery, the pressures of colonialism, and the challenges of modern life have all shaped how African families function today. But even in the face of these challenges, the core remains intact: a deep sense of connection, a commitment to community, and an unshakeable belief in the value of family.

African families in the Caribbean are not monolithic. They vary in language, religion, customs, and traditions. But they share a common thread — a heritage rooted in endurance, creativity, and the ability to transform hardship into strength. Their influence is not confined to history books; it is alive in the way we speak, the way we gather, the way we celebrate, and the way we raise our children.

The Legacy of African Excellence

With such a large percentage of the Caribbean population rooted in African ancestry, it is no surprise that African influence saturates every corner of our culture, from our music and spirituality to our politics, sports, and creative expression. This heritage has produced generations of remarkable individuals whose contributions have shaped not only Jamaica, but the world. Their achievements are not isolated moments of brilliance; they are the flowering of a people who carried resilience in their bones and creativity in their spirit.

The global music landscape was transformed by voices like Bob Marley, Peter Tosh, Bunny Wailer, Dennis Brown, Beres Hammond, and the members of Black Uhuru and Third World—artists who carried the heartbeat of Africa into Reggae, Roots, and Rocksteady. Their songs became anthems of liberation, identity, and spiritual awakening. From the raw energy of Bounty Killer and Shabba Ranks to the lyrical mastery of Buju Banton, Super Cat, and Shaggy, Jamaican music continued to evolve, giving the world Dancehall and a new generation of cultural ambassadors. Damian Marley, Ziggy Marley, and Koffee represent the continuation of this lineage, blending ancestral rhythms with modern expression.

African excellence also shines in the realm of activism and leadership. Marcus Garvey, one of the most influential Pan-Africanists in history, ignited a global movement that reawakened pride in African identity. Paul Bogle, George William Gordon, Samuel Sharpe, and Queen Nanny stand as pillars of resistance—men and women who risked everything to challenge injustice and defend the dignity of their people. Their courage laid the foundation for the freedoms we enjoy today.

In the performing arts, figures like Grace Jones and Trevor Rhone expanded the boundaries of creativity, bringing boldness and innovation to global stages. Heavy D and The Notorious B.I.G., though raised abroad, carried their Jamaican and African heritage into the heart of American music, shaping hip-hop culture in ways that still resonate.

Athletics, too, bears the unmistakable imprint of African families. Usain Bolt, the fastest man in recorded history, stands as a symbol of what happens when natural talent meets discipline, community support, and cultural pride. Courtney Walsh, one of cricket's greatest bowlers, brought honor to the Caribbean through his skill and sportsmanship. Their achievements reflect the strength, endurance, and determination that African families have nurtured for generations.

These individuals—artists, activists, athletes, thinkers—represent only a fraction of the brilliance that has emerged from African families in the Caribbean. Their stories remind us that our heritage is not defined solely by struggle, but by triumph, creativity, and an unbreakable spirit. They are living proof that the African family, despite centuries of disruption, continues to produce excellence that echoes across the world.

To understand the Caribbean family is to understand the African family. Their story is our story. Their legacy is our inheritance. And their resilience continues to shape the identity of the Caribbean in ways both visible and unseen..

Chapter 12:

Indian Families in the Caribbean

The Indian presence in the Caribbean is woven into the region's cultural fabric with a quiet but unmistakable strength. From the moment the first group of East Indians stepped onto Jamaican soil at Old Harbour Bay in 1845, they carried with them a sense of identity that was deeply rooted in ancestry, religion, and tradition. Over the decades, more than 36,000 Indians arrived in Jamaica alone, and tens of thousands more settled in Trinidad and Tobago, Guyana, Suriname, and other islands.

They came as indentured laborers after the abolition of slavery, bringing with them languages, rituals, and family structures that remained largely intact because they arrived as cohesive communities rather than as individuals torn from their homelands. Their family life was anchored in lineage and continuity, with many able to trace their ancestry back to villages in Uttar Pradesh, Bihar, Tamil Nadu, and other regions of India. Even today, Indian families across the Caribbean maintain a strong sense of cultural identity, expressed in their festivals, foods, religious ceremonies, and the values they pass down to their children.

1989: The scenes on Spanish Town Road as dozens of Indian Jamaicans celebrate the ritual of Hussay. The expensive tabernacle, lifted at the center, is blessed in a religious ceremony, carried through the streets, and then dumped into the sea¹.

Indian family life has traditionally been patriarchal, with men seen as providers, decision-makers, and authority figures. Women, though central to the nurturing and emotional life of the home, were often expected to be modest, obedient, and devoted to domestic responsibilities. Marriage was considered a sacred duty, and daughters were raised with the understanding that their honor reflected the honor of the entire family. These values were reinforced through Hindu teachings, which shaped expectations around gender, duty, and generational responsibility. In many households, children were raised to respect their elders, uphold family traditions, and pursue education as a pathway to stability and honor. The belief that children would one day care for their aging parents created a cycle of interdependence that strengthened family bonds across generations.

Over time, Indian families in the Caribbean adapted to new realities while still preserving their cultural roots. Women began pursuing higher education and entering professional fields, even as traditional expectations continued to shape family life. In places like Trinidad and

Guyana, where Indian communities form a significant portion of the population, their influence is visible in politics, business, cuisine, and the arts. In Jamaica, though smaller in number, Indian families have contributed richly to the nation's cultural landscape. Scenes like the Hussay procession on Spanish Town Road in 1989—where Indian Jamaicans carried a beautifully decorated tabernacle through the streets before releasing it into the sea—reflect the enduring presence of Indian religious and cultural traditions. These rituals, passed down through generations, serve as reminders of a heritage that has survived migration, hardship, and change.

Today, Indian families can be found across the Caribbean and throughout the diaspora, from Trinidad and Guyana to Jamaica, the United States, and Canada. Their surnames—Mangaroo, Babooram, Sirjue, Partab, Bhoorasingh, Maragh, Singh, Bandoo, Kissoon, Rambaran, and many others—carry stories of migration, resilience, and cultural pride. Though their numbers vary from island to island, their impact is undeniable. They have built communities that honor their ancestors while embracing the rhythms of Caribbean life. Their presence adds depth to the region's identity, reminding us that the Caribbean is not a single story but a tapestry of many peoples, each bringing their own history, values, and vision of family.

Chapter 13:

Chinese Families in the Caribbean

The story of Chinese families in the Caribbean is one of endurance, quiet strength, and remarkable transformation. Their arrival in the region was not glamorous, nor was it the result of a grand vision for prosperity. Instead, it began with hardship, illness, and the uncertainty of indentureship. Yet from those difficult beginnings emerged communities that would leave an indelible mark on Caribbean society, shaping commerce, culture, and family life in ways that continue to be felt today.

Many Chinese first came to the Caribbean through Panama. In the mid-nineteenth century, laborers were needed to build the railroad connecting Panama City to Colón, a project marked by brutal working conditions and high mortality rates. From there, some were redirected to Jamaica, not by choice but by circumstance. On July 30, 1854, a ship called the Epsom arrived with 267 Chinese immigrants from Hong Kong. They were intended for indentureship, stepping into a world that was unfamiliar, demanding, and often unforgiving. Later that same year, two additional groups—205 workers in total—were sent from Panama to Jamaica after yellow fever ravaged the labor camps. Many were already ill when they arrived, and only a fraction survived after being hospitalized in Kingston. Their journey was marked by loss, but the few who lived went on to plant the earliest seeds of the Chinese Jamaican community.

As the decades passed, more Chinese arrived across the Caribbean, including Trinidad, Guyana, and Suriname. Though they initially came as indentured laborers, they quickly became known for their diligence, discipline, and entrepreneurial spirit. Many transitioned from plantation work to small business ownership, opening shops, bakeries, restaurants, and wholesale establishments that became fixtures in towns and villages. Their presence reshaped the commercial landscape, introducing new foods, new business practices, and a reputation for reliability that earned them respect across communities.

A drawing of the first group of Chinese indentured laborers on their arrival in Jamaica in 1854

Chinese families brought with them a strong sense of cultural identity. They maintained their language, celebrated traditional festivals, and practiced rituals that connected them to their ancestral homeland. Even generations later, many Caribbean Chinese can trace their lineage back to specific provinces in China, preserving family names, stories, and customs with quiet pride. Their homes often reflected a blend of Caribbean warmth and Chinese tradition, creating a unique cultural fusion that enriched the region's diversity.

Family life within Chinese households was traditionally structured around clear roles and expectations. As with Indian families, males were often given preference, encouraged to pursue education, leadership, and financial stability. Sons were seen as carriers of the family name and legacy, while daughters were raised with values of modesty, respect, and responsibility. These expectations were not rooted in harshness but in a cultural framework that emphasized duty, honor, and the continuity of the family line.

Chinese families in the Caribbean were known for their stability and privacy. Their homes were places of order, discipline, and mutual respect. Affection was not always expressed openly, but care was shown through provision, sacrifice, and the quiet acts of service that held the family together. Many practiced the religion of their ancestors—whether traditional Chinese beliefs, Buddhism, or folk practices—while others embraced Catholicism or Anglicanism, faiths that aligned with their preference for solemnity and structure.

Education became a cornerstone of Chinese Caribbean life. Parents encouraged their children to excel academically, seeing education as the pathway to security and advancement. This emphasis produced generations of doctors, pharmacists, business leaders, and professionals who contributed significantly to the development of Caribbean societies. Their success was not accidental; it was the fruit of discipline, sacrifice, and a deep belief in the power of perseverance.

Despite their achievements, Chinese families often lived at the margins of Caribbean society in the early years. They faced cultural misunderstandings, language barriers, and at times, prejudice. Yet they remained steadfast, building communities that were resilient, tightly knit, and deeply committed to progress. Over time, their contributions became impossible to overlook. They helped shape the retail sector, influenced culinary traditions, and added new dimensions to the region's cultural identity.

Today, Chinese families are woven into the Caribbean story with a sense of belonging that spans generations. Their descendants speak with Caribbean accents, celebrate Caribbean holidays, and participate fully in national life, yet many still honor the traditions of their ancestors. This dual identity—rooted in both heritage and homeland—reflects the beauty of Caribbean diversity. It shows how families from distant lands can become integral threads in the fabric of a nation while still preserving the essence of who they are.

The journey of Chinese families in the Caribbean is a proof of their resilience. From the early days of indentureship, marked by illness and uncertainty, to the thriving communities of today, their story reflects the power of determination and cultural pride. They remind us that the Caribbean is not a single narrative but a tapestry of many peoples, each bringing their own history, values, and dreams. And in that tapestry, the Chinese family stands as a quiet but enduring symbol of perseverance, discipline, and the ability to build a life of meaning far from the land of one's birth.

The Legacy of Chinese Caribbean Influence

The influence of Chinese families in the Caribbean is also reflected in the remarkable individuals who have carried this heritage into global spaces. Their surnames—Chai, Chan, Chang, Chen, Chin, Chong, Chung, Chow, Fong, Fung, Hugh, Kong, Lee, Lim, Ling, Lowe, Lyn, Phang, Wan, Wang, Wong, Yap, Young, Yuen, and many others—are woven into the region's history. These names tell stories of migration, perseverance, and the quiet determination that allowed early Chinese immigrants to survive indentureship and build thriving communities. Over generations, their descendants stepped into the world with a confidence shaped by both Caribbean identity and ancestral pride.

Among the most recognizable is Tyson Beckford, whose Jamaican-Chinese heritage contributed to the striking features that made him one of the world's first Black male supermodels. His rise in the fashion industry opened doors for countless others. Naomi Campbell, though often associated with British fashion, also carries Jamaican-Chinese ancestry. Her groundbreaking career as one of the original supermodels reflects the global reach of Caribbean multicultural identity.

The Chin family left an indelible mark on Jamaican music. Vincent and Patricia Chin founded VP Records, a label that became the global home of Reggae and Dancehall. Their work preserved the sound of Jamaica and carried it into international markets, ensuring that Caribbean music would never be confined to the islands. Their legacy continues through generations of artists whose careers were shaped by the platform VP Records created.

Tessanne Chin brought the richness of her Jamaican-Chinese heritage to the world stage through her music. Her powerful voice and effortless blend of cultural influences earned her international acclaim and reminded audiences everywhere of the depth of Caribbean talent. In public life, Delroy Chuck has served Jamaica with distinction, reflecting the enduring commitment of Chinese Jamaican families to civic leadership and national development.

The creative world also bears the imprint of this heritage. Sarah Cooper, the comedian and writer whose sharp satire gained global attention, draws from her Jamaican-Chinese background to shape her unique voice. Ayesha Curry, known for her work in entertainment, authorship, and entrepreneurship, carries this lineage as well, blending Caribbean warmth with global influence in her public persona and business ventures.

In the realm of business, Michael Lee-Chin stands as one of the Caribbean's most successful entrepreneurs. His rise from modest beginnings to international prominence reflects the discipline, ambition, and strategic thinking often nurtured within Chinese Caribbean households. His philanthropy and investments continue to impact Jamaica and the wider region.

Even in music, the multicultural tapestry of the Caribbean is evident. Sean Paul, whose heritage includes Chinese Jamaican roots, became one of the most globally recognized Dancehall artists of his generation. His success reflects the fusion of cultures that defines Caribbean identity and demonstrates how Chinese ancestry has quietly shaped the sound and spirit of the region.

Together, these individuals embody the resilience, discipline, and cultural pride that Chinese families brought to the Caribbean. Their achievements are not isolated successes but the natural outgrowth of communities that valued education, hard work, and the preservation of heritage. Through them, the story of Chinese Caribbean families continues to unfold—rich, influential, and deeply interwoven with the identity of the region.

Chapter 14:

Jewish Families in the Caribbean

The story of Jewish families in the Caribbean is one of quiet endurance, deep faith, and remarkable adaptation. Their presence in Jamaica and across the region stretches back nearly five centuries, beginning during one of the darkest periods in European history—the Spanish Inquisition. Around 1530, Jews fleeing persecution, torture, and forced conversion sought refuge wherever they could find it. Many of them found their way to the Caribbean, including Jamaica, hoping for a place where they could live without fear and practice their faith in peace.

The first Jewish arrivals were primarily Sephardic Jews from Spain and Portugal. Some had even traveled with Christopher Columbus, while others later assisted British forces in capturing Jamaica from the Spanish. Under Spanish rule, Jews were forced to live in secrecy, practicing their faith behind closed doors and hiding their identity to avoid punishment. But when the English took control of Jamaica in 1655, everything changed. For the first time, Jews were allowed to worship openly, build synagogues, and establish communities rooted in their traditions. This shift marked the beginning of a vibrant Jewish presence on the island.

By 1700, the Jewish community had grown significantly. Historical records note that around 400 Jews lived in Jamaica at that time, owning several plantations and participating actively in commerce. By 1720, Jews made up nearly 18 percent of Kingston's population—a remarkable figure that speaks to their early influence on the island's economic and social life. Their contributions were not limited to business; they helped shape the cultural and civic landscape of Jamaica during its formative years.

Another wave of Jewish migration came in 1656, when Lord Protector Oliver Cromwell granted Rabbi Menasseh ben Israel permission for Jews to settle in England and, by extension, in English colonies. This opened the door for more Jewish families to make their way to Jamaica, seeking stability and the freedom to practice their faith. For a time, the community flourished. Synagogues were built, businesses expanded, and Jewish families became an integral part of Jamaican society.

Source: The Jewish Museum London.

Yet, like many immigrant communities, the Jewish population in Jamaica experienced periods of decline. By the mid-1900s, the number of practicing Jews had fallen to around 1,300.

Political unrest in the 1970s prompted another wave of emigration, as many families left in search of safety and economic opportunity. Today, only about 200 practicing Jews remain on the island, according to the ANU Museum of the Jewish People and the Joshua Project. Their numbers may be small, but their historical footprint is vast.

What is less visible — but deeply significant — is the number of Jamaicans who carry Jewish ancestry without even knowing it. Scholars estimate that approximately 424,000 Jamaicans are descendants of Jewish settlers. Over generations, Jewish families intermarried with African, European, and mixed-heritage communities, blending their lineage into the broader Jamaican population. Because children traditionally took their father's surname, many Jewish names became woven into Jamaican identity, even when the religious practices faded. This blending makes it difficult to trace distinct Jewish family customs today, but the heritage remains embedded in the island's history.

Jewish families in Jamaica were known for their strong emphasis on education, entrepreneurship, and community cohesion. Their synagogues served not only as places of worship but as centers of learning and cultural preservation. Even as many families migrated, the values they carried—discipline, resilience, and devotion to family—continued to influence the generations that followed. Their presence enriched Jamaica's cultural mosaic, adding another layer to the island's identity as a place shaped by many peoples and traditions.

Although the practicing Jewish community is now small, its legacy lives on in the architecture of old synagogues, in family names scattered across the island, and in the stories of ancestors who crossed oceans seeking freedom. Their journey is a reminder that the Caribbean has long been a refuge for those fleeing persecution, and that its strength lies in its ability to absorb, adapt, and honor the cultures that take root on its shores.

Jewish families brought with them a deep sense of faith, a commitment to community, and a determination to survive against all odds. These qualities allowed them to thrive in Jamaica despite periods of hardship, migration, and change. Their story is one of quiet perseverance — less visible than some of the larger cultural groups, but no less significant. They remind us that family identity is not always loud or dominant; sometimes it is carried in memory, in names, in values, and in the subtle threads that bind a people to their past.

Legacy of Jewish Influence in the Caribbean

Jewish heritage in the Caribbean is often quiet, woven into surnames, family stories, and the subtle threads of ancestry that many Jamaicans carry without realizing it. Names such as Abrahams, Alexander, Andrade, Barrett, Babb, Bent, Carvalho, Codner, DeCosta, De La Roche, Da Silva, De Souza, De Cohen, De Leon, Delisser, DeMercado, Eben, Fuertado, Henriques, Ibanez, Isaacs, Levy, Levell, Lindo, Lyon, Machado,

Marish, Matalon, Mendes, Myers, Magnus, Nunes, Pimentel, Rodriques, and Sangster reflect the long presence of Sephardic Jews who settled on the island from as early as the sixteenth century. These families blended into Jamaican society over generations, contributing to commerce, politics, the arts, and national development, even as many of their descendants became part of the wider African population through intermarriage and cultural integration.

This heritage is visible in the lives of several notable Jamaicans whose influence has reached far beyond the island's shores. Bob Marley, perhaps the most globally recognized Jamaican, carried Jewish ancestry through his father, Norval Marley, a Syrian Jew. His music, rooted in liberation and spiritual consciousness, became a universal language that connected people across cultures. Chris Blackwell, founder of Island Records, played a pivotal role in bringing Reggae to the world, shaping the careers of artists like Marley, Tosh, and U2. His work stands as one of the most significant cultural exports in Jamaican history.

The Matalon family, represented by figures such as Joseph Mayer Matalon, contributed significantly to Jamaica's business landscape, particularly through WIHCON Homes and other major enterprises. The Henriques lineage produced talents like Sean Paul Francis Henriques, whose global success in Reggae and Dancehall reflects the multicultural tapestry of Jamaican identity. Jewish influence also shaped civic leadership, with mayors such as Richard Stern, Ernest Altamont da Costa, and Eli Matalon guiding Kingston through pivotal periods of growth and modernization.

Diplomacy and literature also bear the imprint of Jewish Jamaican heritage. Sir Neville Noel Ashenheim became Jamaica's first ambassador to Washington, representing the newly independent nation with distinction. Jorge Ricardo Isaacs, author of the celebrated novel *María*, carried Jamaican Jewish ancestry into Latin American literary history. Architecture, too, was shaped by this community through figures like Rudolph Henriques, whose work contributed to Kingston's cultural landscape.

The arts flourished under the hands of Jewish descendants such as Isaac Mendes Belisario, a nineteenth-century painter whose depictions of Jamaican life remain invaluable historical records, and Daniel Lopez Laguna, a poet whose writings reflect the spiritual and cultural complexity of the Sephardic diaspora. Even the story of George Stiebel, Jamaica's first Black millionaire and the visionary behind Devon House, intersects with Jewish lineage through his father's heritage. His rise from humble beginnings to national prominence embodies the resilience that defines so much of Jamaica's multicultural history. Actor and activist Harry Belafonte, whose global influence in music, film, and civil rights is legendary, also carried Jewish Jamaican ancestry through his mother's lineage.

Jewish presence in Jamaica is also reflected in institutions such as Hillel Academy, a school founded with Jewish roots that continues to serve families from diverse backgrounds. While it does not overtly display its origins, it remains a quiet testament to the community's longstanding commitment to education, cultural preservation, and the nurturing of future generations.

Together, these individuals and families illustrate how Jewish heritage—though often understated—has shaped Jamaica's cultural, political, and artistic identity in profound ways. Their stories reveal a legacy of resilience, creativity, and contribution that continues to echo through the island's history and into its modern life.

Chapter 15:

Conclusion

The Caribbean family did not emerge from a single story. It was shaped by crossings and collisions, by forced arrivals and chosen migrations, by the quiet persistence of culture and the unyielding will to survive. Every group that came to these shores—whether by chains, contract, or choice—brought with them a way of seeing the world, a way of raising children, a way of holding community together. Over centuries, these ways intertwined, sometimes gently, sometimes painfully, until they formed the living mosaic we now call the Caribbean family.

Understanding this history allows us to see our families with new eyes. We recognize the echoes of Africa in our communal bonds, our music, and our resilience. We see the imprint of India in our discipline, our devotion to family, and our respect for tradition. We notice the influence of Chinese households in our business culture, our emphasis on education, and our quiet determination. We acknowledge the Jewish presence in our names, our institutions, and the entrepreneurial spirit that helped shape our early towns and cities. Each group left something behind — something that still breathes through our customs, our language, and our sense of identity.

The Caribbean family has endured hardship, separation, migration, and reinvention. Yet it remains one of the strongest social structures in our region. It adapts. It bends. It rebuilds. It carries memory in its bones and hope in its hands. And even when scattered across oceans, it finds ways to remain connected.

As we look to the future, may we honor the stories that brought us here. May we recognize the beauty in our diversity and the strength in our shared history. And may we continue to build families rooted in dignity, compassion, and the understanding that we are, and have always been, a people shaped by many journeys.

REFERENCES

Barrow, C., (1998). Family in the
Caribbean: Themes and perspectives.
Jamaica, Ian Randle Publishers, 1998. p.
1 - 46

Barrow, C., Reddock, R., (2001). Caribbean
sociology: Introductory readings.
Jamaica, Ian Randle Publishers, 2001. p.
418-425.

Lambert, R., (2020). Jews in Jamaica.
Jewish Museum, London.

Macaulay, M.M., (2014, June 23). A
common-law spouse's entitlement.
Jamaica Observer.

Mehrotra, A., (2005). Gender and family.

Stewart, M., (2002). Changing role of
fathers. 4th Caribbean Early Childhood
Development Conference.

Stewart, T., M., (2005). The family. Family
Life Education Project, Ministry of
Education, Kingston, Jamaica

Tortello, R. (2005). Out Of Many Cultures
the People Who Came: The Arrival of
The Indians.

.

Remember, "the heights by great men reached and kept were not attained by sudden flight, but they, while their companions slept, were toiling upward in the night." – Henry Wadsworth Longfellow.

ABOUT THE AUTHOR

Minister Denise N. Fyffe

… is an author, educator, and Christian minister whose work centers on emotional wellness, family life, and spiritual growth. Born and raised in Jamaica, she carries the wisdom of a culture rooted in community, resilience, and faith. Her upbringing continues to shape her perspective on family, identity, and the importance of raising children with intention and grace.

With more than a fifteen years of experience in writing, teaching, and ministry leadership, Denise has dedicated her life to helping individuals and families navigate the complexities of modern living. She is the founder of RTCLM Academy and Jamaica Pen Publishers, where she mentors writers, supports emerging leaders, and develops resources that strengthen homes and communities.

Her books blend cultural insight, spiritual grounding, and practical guidance, offering readers clarity in a world that often feels overwhelming. Through her work, she encourages families to build strong foundations, embrace emotional wellness, and lead with compassion in a fast-changing digital age.

Denise continues to write, teach, and minister with a heart for service and a commitment to empowering families across the world..

RECOMMENDED BOOKS

All books are available at online book retailers,
including Lulu.com and Amazon.com.

Thank you for reading this book.

It means so much that you have taken the time out of your busy schedule. Nothing makes us happier than knowing that someone is reading, and hopefully enjoying, what took us many months, even years, to create.

Please stay with us on this journey. We welcome your feedback, opinions, and suggestions about the book. We would appreciate a few lines of review on the website where you purchased this book.

You can also write us a note at Jamaica Pen Publishing on Facebook, or Twitter or contact us via our website.